Sue Quinn

photographs by Victoria Wall Harris

hardie grant books

CONTENTS

WHAT IS A SUPERFOOD?

Superfood is a term often exploited by food manufacturers to make products seem more nutritious than they actually are. Sometimes these products lack the scientific evidence to support their alleged health benefits and are no more than fads. This is a shame. Marketing hype aside, there is hard scientific research to show that some foods contain exceptional levels of nutrients that promote good health and protect the human body against disease. These are the *superfoods* I have focused on in this book.

Finding a standard measure of what constitutes a *superfood* is, however, complicated. A number of rating systems have been developed around the world that rank foods according to their nutrient density, the measure of nutrients per calorie. The problem is that these systems are not consistent. For example, some use different sets of essential nutrients as the basis for the rating. What's more, nutrient density is not the only important factor. For example, there are thousands of phytochemicals that appear to have the potential to protect against a range of diseases, but these are not included in nutrient density measures because they have not been established as essential for bodily function.

After researching various rating systems, I have devised my own list of powerhouse foods (see pages 10–16) that contain exceptionally high levels of vitamins, phytochemicals and other nutrients that are strongly associated with good health and reduced risk of chronic disease. The superfoods that appear on this list are emboldened within each recipe's ingredients list, so that they can be identified easily.

The list is by no means exhaustive, but provides a cross-section of superfoods in different food groups to help you load your diet with as much goodness as possible.

SUPERFOOD TERMS YOU SHOULD KNOW

ANTIOXIDANTS

Fruit, vegetables & grains are the richest sources.

Chemicals that block the activity of **free radicals**.

Protect cells from damage.

CAROTENOIDS

Carotenoids give carrots, squash & other fruit & vegetables their orange colour.

A group of **phytochemicals** that includes carotene, beta-carotene & lycopene.

Powerful antioxidants.

FLAVONOIDS

Found in berries, tree fruits, nuts, beans & vegetables among others.

A large group of **phytochemicals**.

Linked to longevity & reduced risk of heart disease. Powerful antioxidants.

FOLATE

Particularly high levels in dark green leafy vegetables.

A type of **Vitamin B**, also known as **folic acid**.

Vital for growth.

FREE RADICALS

Formed naturally in the body; also in the environment, for example cigarette smoke & pollution.

Reactive chemicals that have the potential to damage cells.

Can lead to age-related conditions like cancer, diabetes & heart disease.

A basic knowledge of the common nutritional terms listed below will make it easier to understand the benefits of superfoods.

GLUCOSINOLATES

Found in cruciferous vegetables like rocket, bok choy, cabbage, kale & watercress.

Sulphur-containing chemicals.

Thought to inhibit the development of some cancers.

LYCOPENES

Found in fruit & vegetables such as tomatoes & pink grapefruit.

A group of **phytochemicals**.

Powerful antioxidants.

PHYTOCHEMICALS

A large group of non-essential plant-based nutrients with disease protective and preventative properties.

Certain types referred to as **antioxidants, flavonoids, carotenoids & polyphenols**.

May protect against cancer, also linked to lower blood pressure, improved vision & lower cholesterol.

VITAMIN A

A broad group of nutrients that includes retinoids (in animal foods) & carotenoids (in plant foods).

In this book, Vitamin A refers to all the combined forms contained in a food.

May protect against cancer, also works as an anti-inflammatory.

VITAMIN C

One of the best-known antioxidants.

VITAMIN E

A generic term for a family of nutrients with powerful antioxidant benefits.

VITAMIN K

Well known for its role in helping blood to clot; also promotes bone strengthening.

SUPERFOODS TABLE

The following list of superfoods is drawn from sources including the ANDI (Aggregate Nutrient Density Index) system, the US Centers for Disease Control and Prevention's index of fruit and vegetables ranked by nutrient density[1], and the 100 richest dietary sources of antioxidants as published in the European Journal of Clinical Nutrition[2]. Some other foods identified as having particular health benefits are also included. The foods are listed in no particular order *NOTE: the milks, wakame, tahini, miso etc. that are emboldened within the recipes are forms of the superfoods that are listed in the table.*

GREEN VEGETABLES	KEY NUTRIENTS & POTENTIAL HEALTH BENEFITS
mustard greens	**Vitamins K, A & C** Lowers cholesterol; cancer protection
turnip greens	**Vitamins A, K, C & folate, calcium, flavonoids** Protects against cancer and cardiovascular problems; anti-inflammatory
collard greens	**Vitamins K, A & C, manganese** Protects against cancer and cardiovascular problems; lowers cholesterol; anti-inflammatory
beet greens	**Vitamins K, A & C, calcium, magnesium** Eye health; comprehensive nourishment

Vitamins K, C & A
Protects against cancer, osteoporosis and Alzheimer's disease

watercress

Vitamins K, A & C, manganese, glucosinolates, flavonoids
Lowers cholesterol; cancer protection; anti-inflammatory

kale

Vitamins K, A & C, magnesium, flavonoids
Anti-inflammatory; regulates blood sugar; cancer protection; supports bone health

Swiss chard

Vitamins K, C & A, potassium, glucosinolates
Cancer protection; anti-inflammatory

bok choy

Vitamins K, C & B6, glucosinolates
Cancer protection; anti-inflammatory; lowers cholesterol

cabbage

Vitamins K, A, & folate, manganese, carotenoids
Protects against cancer, anti-inflammatory; supports bone health

spinach

Vitamins K, A, C & folate
Protects against cancer; supports digestive health; lowers cholesterol

chicory

Vitamins K, A, C & folate, carotenoids
Cancer protection

rocket

Vitamins K, A & folate, flavonoids, carotenoids
Protects against cardiovascular problems; lowers cholesterol

Romaine lettuce

OTHER VEGETABLES	KEY NUTRIENTS & POTENTIAL HEALTH BENEFITS

 radish

Vitamin C, carotenoids
Cancer protection; anti-inflammatory; boosts immunity

 turnip

Vitamin C
Cancer protection; anti-inflammatory; boosts immunity

 artichoke hearts

Vitamins C, K & folate, fibre
Lowers cholesterol; anti-inflammatory; supports digestive health

 carrots

Vitamins A, K & biotin (B7), carotenoids
Protects against cardiovascular disease and cancer; supports eye health

 acorn squash

Vitamin A, C & B6, fibre, carotenoids
Anti-inflammatory; regulates blood sugar; protects against heart disease and cancer

 red, yellow & orange pepper

Vitamin C, B6 & A, flavonoids, carotenoids
Regulates blood sugar; protects against heart disease & cancer

 cauliflower

Vitamin C, K & folate
Protection against heart disease and cancer; anti-inflammatory; supports digestive health

 swede

Vitamin C, potassium, carotenoids, fibre
Protects again cancer, heart and bone disease, supports digestive health

KEY NUTRIENTS & POTENTIAL HEALTH BENEFITS	NUTS & SEEDS	
Omega-3 fatty acids, fibre Protects against cancer and heart disease; lowers cholesterol; supports digestive health; eases post-menopausal symptoms	flaxseeds	
Vitamins E & B-group, manganese, copper, carotenoids, fibre Lowers cholesterol; protects against heart disease, cancer and infection; promotes healthy skin	pecans	
Vitamins C & B-group, copper, manganese, fibre Protects against heart disease; lowers cholesterol; supports bone health	chestnuts	
Vitamins E & B-group, manganese, copper, fibre Protects against heart disease and cancer; lowers cholesterol; promotes healthy skin	hazelnuts	
Copper, manganese, calcium Relief for rheumatoid arthritis; supports vascular, respiratory and bone health; protects against cancer and osteoporosis	sesame seeds	
Vitamins E & B-group, copper, manganese, selenium Lowers cholesterol, prevents heart disease, reduces blood sugar levels	sunflower seeds	
B-group vitamins, copper, manganese, flavonoids Protects against heart disease, stroke, cancer and Alzheimer's disease	peanuts	
Omega-3 fatty acids, manganese, calcium, phosphorous, fibre Limited research but may support cardiovascular health	chia seeds	

FRUIT	KEY NUTRIENTS & POTENTIAL HEALTH BENEFITS

 cranberries

Vitamin C, flavonoids, other phytochemicals, fibre
Protection against urinary tract infection, cardiovascular disease and cell damage; anti-inflammatory

 blackberries

Vitamins C, K & folate, manganese, flavonoids, fibre
Protects against cancer and premature ageing; regulates blood sugar; anti-inflammatory

 strawberries

Vitamin C, manganese, flavonoids, phytochemicals, fibre
Protection against heart disease and cancer; anti-inflammatory; regulates blood sugar

 raspberries

Vitamin C, manganese, flavonoids, phytochemicals, fibre
Regulates blood sugar and supports weight loss; protects against cancer

 blueberries

Vitamin K & C, manganese, flavonoids
Protects against cardiovascular disease, cancer and memory loss; supports eye health; regulates blood sugar

 pink & red grapefruit, lemon, lime

Vitamin C, lycopene (pink & red grapefruit only), flavonoids
Protects against cancer, rheumatoid arthritis and cell damage; supports the immune system; anti-inflammatory

 orange

Vitamin C, flavonoids, fibre
Lowers cholesterol; protects against cancer, heart disease and rheumatoid arthritis; supports immune system

 sweet cherry

Vitamins A & C, flavonoids, phytochemicals
Protects against cancer and cardiovascular disease; anti-inflammatory; calms nervous system

black plum

Vitamin C, flavonoids, phytochemicals
Protection against cell damage; regulates blood sugar and supports weight loss; improves iron absorption

Vitamins C & A
Protection against cancer, anti-viral, promotes
good circulation

black elderberry

Vitamin C, carotenoids, flavonoids
Protects against cancer, premature ageing and
neurological disease

ariona berry

Vitamin C & B-group, flavonoids, carotenoids
Protects against cardiovascular disease and cancer; supports
bone health; lowers cholesterol; supports weight loss

tomato

Vitamins C & B2, selenium, iron, carotenoids, fibre
Limited research but may offer cancer protection and
support immune system; anti-inflammatory

goji berries

Vitamin A, flavonoids and other phytochemicals
Limited research but like other dark berries may protect
against cardiovascular disease and support weight loss

acai berries

KEY NUTRIENTS & POTENTIAL
HEALTH BENEFITS

BEANS

Molybdenum (essential mineral), folate and fibre
Lowers cholesterol, regulates blood sugar, protects against
heart disease

pinto/kidney/red
beans/lentils

Protein, iron, magnesium and calcium
Protection against cancer and heart disease, promotes
bone health

tofu/edamame/soya

| OTHER | KEY NUTRIENTS & POTENTIAL HEALTH BENEFITS |

 kmaca powder — **Vitamin C & B-group, minerals, phytochemicals**
Limited research but said to boost energy and support hormone balance

 cocoa — **B-group vitamins, minerals, flavonoids**
Antidepressant; mild stimulant; reduces risk of stroke and heart attack, aids weight loss

 mackerel — **Vitamin D & B-group, omega-3 fatty acids**
Reduces risk of heart disease; lowers cholesterol; anti-inflammatory; reduces blood pressure

 salmon — **Vitamin D & B-group, selenium and omega-3 fatty acids**
Protects against cardiovascular disease and cancer; protects joints and promotes eye health

 seaweed — **Vitamin C, iodine, minerals, phytochemicals**
Anti-inflammatory; lowers cholesterol; protects against cancer

 basil — **Vitamin K, flavonoids**
Regulates blood sugar; lowers cholesterol; antibacterial

 coriander (seeds & leaves) — **Vitamin K, flavonoids and other phytochemicals**
Regulates blood sugar; lowers cholesterol; antibacterial

TOP SOURCES OF VITAMINS IN SUPERFOODS

Use the information provided below to identify which superfoods are the best sources for key vitamins[3].

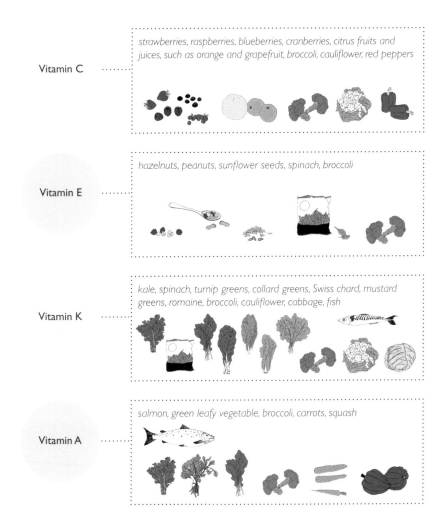

Vitamin C

strawberries, raspberries, blueberries, cranberries, citrus fruits and juices, such as orange and grapefruit, broccoli, cauliflower, red peppers

Vitamin E

hazelnuts, peanuts, sunflower seeds, spinach, broccoli

Vitamin K

kale, spinach, turnip greens, collard greens, Swiss chard, mustard greens, romaine, broccoli, cauliflower, cabbage, fish

Vitamin A

salmon, green leafy vegetable, broccoli, carrots, squash

BREAKFAST

Start the day as you mean to go on with these powerhouse breakfast ideas. Nutrient-packed smoothies provide a quick shot of goodness for those in a hurry, while bowls, pots and toast are perfect for fuelling up with super seeds, berries and nuts.

Chocca smoothie • Wonder smoothie
Berry blast smoothie • Strawberry superspread
Spiced power pot • Cherry crush toasts
Get-the-glow porridge • Super muesli

CHOCCA SMOOTHIE

*Serves: 1 person * Time: 5 minutes*

CONTAINS

Vitamins B-group, C & E minerals, flavonoids,
phytochemicals, omega-3 fatty acids, fibre, protein,
iron, magnesium, manganese, phosphorous,
selenium, copper & calcium

YOU NEED

250ml milk of choice, such as dairy, **soya** or **flax**, plus extra to taste
1 small banana • ½ tablespoon **cocoa powder** or **cocoa nibs**
½ tablespoon **maca powder** • 1 teaspoon each **flaxseeds, chia seeds** and
sunflower seeds • 2 tablespoons rolled oats • honey or agave, to taste

Place all the ingredients in a bender and blitz on high power until smooth and
creamy, adding more milk if needed to achieve the desired consistency.

WONDER SMOOTHIE

Serves: 1 person ✳ *Time: 5 minutes*

CONTAINS
Vitamins A, C, K, folate, manganese, glucosinolates,
flavonoids, carotenoids & fibre

YOU NEED
1 pear, cored and chopped with skin on • 1 apple, cored and chopped with skin on
2 small handfuls of **kale** • 1 small handful of **spinach**
juice of 1 **lime** • 80ml **orange juice** • ½ teaspoon grated fresh ginger

POTENTIAL
BENEFITS

protects against *cancer,
cell damage, heart disease,
rheumatoid arthritis*
• **lowers** *cholesterol*
• **supports** *bone health,
immune system*
• *anti-inflammatory*

Place all the ingredients in a blender and blitz on high power until smooth.
Depending on the power of your blender, you might need to push the mixture
through a sieve to achieve a smoother consistency.

BERRY BLAST SMOOTHIE

Serves: 1 person ✳ *Time: 5 minutes*

CONTAINS

Vitamins A, C, K & folate, manganese, omega-3
fatty acids, flavonoids, phytochemicals, calcium,
phosphorous, protein, iron, magnesium, fibre

YOU NEED

45g **blackberries** • 45g **blueberries** • 45g **raspberries**

60ml **acai juice** • ¼ teaspoon grated fresh ginger

2 teaspoons **chia seeds** • 250ml **flax, soya** or dairy milk

1 tablespoon runny honey, or more to taste • 1 tablespoon natural yoghurt

Place all the ingredients in a blender and blitz on high power for 2 minutes, or until
combined and the seeds are completely broken down. Push through a sieve
if necessary to achieve the desired consistency. Taste, and add more honey
if needed, before serving.

STRAWBERRY SUPERSPREAD

Makes: about 275g ∗ Time: 15 minutes, plus 10 minutes to thicken

CONTAINS
Vitamin C, manganese, flavonoids, phytochemicals,
omega-3 fatty acids, manganese, calcium,
phosphorous, fibre

YOU NEED
500g **strawberries**, hulled and quartered • 2–3 tablespoons runny honey
a squeeze of **lemon** • 3 tablespoons **chia seeds**, plus extra if needed

Place the strawberries in a pan and mash with a potato masher. Cook over a
medium–low heat, stirring, until the berries release their juice. Stir in the honey and
lemon, increase the heat and simmer for 10 minutes, or until thickened. Remove
from the heat and stir in the chia seeds. Set aside for 10 minutes – if the mixture
hasn't thickened into a jam add more chia seeds and/or return to the heat for a few
more minutes. Cool, then store in an airtight container in the fridge.

SPICED POWER POT

*Serves: 1 person * Time: 50 minutes, plus 10 minutes cooling*

CONTAINS

Vitamin A, B-group, C & E, fibre, carotenoids, copper,
manganese, selenium

YOU NEED

300g **acorn squash**, deseeded and cut into large chunks (with skin still on)

a generous pinch of cinnamon • a scant pinch of nutmeg

½ tablespoon unsalted butter • 1 tablespoon rolled oats or spelt flakes

½ tablespoon **sunflower seeds** • ½ tablespoon pumpkin seeds

pinch of fine sea salt • ½ tablespoon runny honey • 150g Greek-style yoghurt

Preheat the oven to 180°C/350°F/Gas 4. Roast the squash for 30–40 minutes until tender. Cool slightly, then scrape the flesh into a food processor, add the cinnamon and nutmeg and purée. Set aside to cool. Heat the butter in a small frying pan and add the oats or spelt, seeds and salt. Stir-fry over a medium-high heat until lightly toasted – don't burn the seeds. Add the honey and stir-fry for 1 minute until sticky. Cool on a plate, then break into pieces. To serve, layer the yoghurt, squash purée and seeds in a small glass jar or bowl.

CHERRY CRUSH TOASTS

*Serves: 1 person * Time: 15 minutes*

CONTAINS

Vitamins A, B-group, C, E & K, flavonoids,
phytochemicals, copper, manganese, selenium, calcium,
omega-3 fatty acids, phosphorous, fibre

YOU NEED

125g **sweet cherries**, fresh or frozen, pitted • 1 tablespoon runny honey
or agave syrup • 1 tablespoon **lemon juice** • 2 **basil leaves**
1–2 slices **seedy bread** • 2–3 tablespoons labneh (cream cheese
will work as an alternative) • **sesame seeds**, for sprinkling

Place the cherries, honey or agave syrup and lemon juice in a pan and lightly crush with a potato masher. Bring to a gentle simmer, then reduce the heat to low, cover and cook for 5 minutes. Tear the basil leaves into the pan and gently simmer uncovered for a further 5 minutes until the juices reduce to a syrup. Meanwhile, toast the bread and spread with the labneh. To serve, spoon the cherries and sauce over the labneh and sprinkle with sesame seeds.

GET-THE-GLOW PORRIDGE

Serves: 1 person ∗ *Time: 20 minutes*

CONTAINS
Vitamins B-group, C, E & K, manganese, flavonoids,
carotenoids, phytochemicals, copper, selenium,
omega-3 fatty acids, fibre

YOU NEED
40g **raspberries** • 40g **blueberries**
300–400ml **flax**, almond or dairy milk, plus extra if needed, and to serve
20g rolled oats • 20g quinoa flakes • 1 tablespoon **sunflower seeds**
1 teaspoon **flax seeds** • pinch of fine sea salt • ½ teaspoon ground cinnamon
1 tablespoon runny honey • chopped **pecans or hazelnuts**, to serve

Blitz the berries in a mini food processor or blender then set aside. Gently heat the
milk in a pan and set aside, keeping it warm. Combine the oats, quinoa and seeds
in a pan and cook, stirring, over a medium–high heat until the mixture smells nutty
and toasted. Add half the warm milk, stir briskly, then the cinnamon and honey.
Cook gently for 15 minutes, stirring, and adding the remaining warm milk, plus
extra cold milk if needed, to maintain the desired consistency. Pour into a bowl,
swirl the berry sauce in and sprinkle with nuts.

SUPER MUESLI

Makes: about 700g or serves 8 people ∗ *Time: 5 minutes*

CONTAINS

Vitamins B-group, C & E, manganese, copper,
carotenoids, omega-3 fatty acids, calcium,
phosphorous, fibre, selenium, iron

YOU NEED

180g rolled oats • 180g quinoa flakes • 80g **pecan nuts**, chopped roughly

3 tablespoons **chia seeds** • 70g dried mango, chopped roughly

30g **goji berries** • 2 teaspoons ground cinnamon

pinch of fine sea salt • 70g dried apricots, chopped roughly

30g pumpkin seeds • 2 tablespoons **sesame seeds**

In a large mixing bowl, stir together all the ingredients until evenly distributed.
Store in an airtight container.

SALADS, SOUPS & SMALL PLATES

Salads and soups are ideal for squeezing as much goodness into one bowl as possible, and the recipes here are brimming with antioxidants and other nutrients. There are also plates of tasty goodness that you can keep to yourself or share — if you want to.

Go-to cleanse salad •Super bowl salad
Vibrant bread salad • Sesame crunch bowl
Superslaw • Goodness bowl • Zingy cheat's pizza
• Tofu bites & punchy pickles • Sunshine soup
Soup soother • Creamy comfort soup • Peanut
hummus • Vitaboost frittata

GO-TO CLEANSE SALAD

Serves: 1 person • *Time: 5 minutes*

CONTAINS
Vitamins A, B-group C, E & K, manganese, copper,
selenium, flavonoids, fibre

YOU NEED

½ tablespoon chopped **blanched hazelnuts** • ½ tablespoons **sunflower seeds**

½ teaspoon Nigella seeds • a pinch of sea salt • 50g **watercress** or **upland cress**

(weighed without thick stalks) • 1 tablespoon **lemon juice**

3 tablespoons extra virgin olive oil

POTENTIAL BENEFITS

protects against *heart disease, cancer, osteoporosis, Alzheimer's disease, rheumatoid arthritis & cell damage*
• **lowers** *cholesterol*
• **regulates** *blood sugar levels*
• **supports** *the immune system & healthy skin levels*
• *anti-inflammatory*

For the salad, place the nuts, seeds and salt in a frying pan and toast, stirring, until aromatic. Be careful not to burn. Set aside to cool. Place the watercress in a salad bowl. Gently toss with lemon juice and olive oil and scatter with the seed mixture. Serve immediately.

SUPER BOWL SALAD

Serves: 1 person as a main • Time: 10 minutes

CONTAINS

Vitamins A, B-group, C, E & K, carotenoids,
manganese, glucosinolates, flavonoids, copper,
selenium, iron, fibre

YOU NEED

3 tablespoons olive oil • 1 teaspoon **lemon juice** • 1 teaspoon honey
½ garlic clove, finely chopped • sea salt flakes • freshly ground black pepper
100g **kale leaves**, finely sliced • 70g **cabbage**, shredded • 1 medium **carrot**, grated
1 avocado, stoned, peeled and sliced • 3 tablespoons **sunflower seeds**
80g **blueberries** • 2 tablespoons **goji berries** or **aronia berries**, or a mixture

Whisk together the oil, lemon juice, honey, garlic and salt and pepper. Set aside.
Place the remaining ingredients in a salad bowl. Toss with
the dressing and serve immediately.

VIBRANT BREAD SALAD

Serves: 4 people as a side • Time: 20 minutes

CONTAINS
Vitamins A, B-group, C & K, copper, manganese,
calcium, glucosinolates, flavonoids, carotenoids

YOU NEED
2 pitta bread • 1 garlic clove, cut in half

2 tablespoons olive oil, plus extra for brushing and drizzling

3 tablespoons **tahini** • 2 tablespoon **lemon juice**, plus extra to taste

1 teaspoon sumac (or smoked sweet paprika) • sea salt flakes

freshly ground black pepper • a large handful of **baby kale** • 50g **watercress**

240g **tomatoes**, chopped • 100g **radishes**, chopped

POTENTIAL
BENEFITS

protects against *cancer,
cardiovascular disease,
rheumatoid arthritis, cell damage,
Alzheimer's disease & osteoporosis*
• **lowers** *cholesterol* • **supports**
*vascular, respiratory, bone health,
immune system & weight loss*
• *anti-inflammatory*

Preheat the oven to 180°C/350°F/Gas 4. Rub the pitta on both sides with the cut garlic. Brush with olive oil, cut into bite-sized pieces, and place on a baking tray. Bake for 10 minutes until starting to crisp. To make the dressing, crush the remaining garlic into a screw-top jar and add the oil, tahini, lemon, sumac and 4 tablespoons cold water. Season with salt and pepper, shake vigorously and set aside. Place all the remaining ingredients in a salad bowl, add the toasted pitta, and toss with enough of the dressing to coat. Serve immediately.

SESAME CRUNCH BOWL

Serves: 1 person • Time: 15 minutes, plus a few minutes cooling

CONTAINS
Vitamins A, C & K, copper, manganese, calcium, folate,
carotenoids, glucosinolates, flavonoids, potassium

YOU NEED
3 tablespoons toasted **sesame oil** • 75g shiitake mushrooms, sliced

1 tablespoon sake • ½ tablespoon mirin • sea salt flakes

freshly ground black pepper • 2 teaspoons rice wine vinegar

½ tablespoon fish sauce • ½ teaspoon grated fresh ginger

50g mixed leaves such as **rocket**, **baby kale** and **baby mustard leaves**

1 or 2 heads of **bok choy**, about 70g, leaves separated and large leaves halved

1 large, or a few baby, **radishes**, about 40g, finely sliced

Heat 1 tablespoon of the sesame oil in a frying pan and fry the mushrooms until
they are soft and releasing their juices. Add the sake and mirin and let the liquid
bubble away, then season with salt and pepper. Set aside to cool a little. Place the
remaining sesame oil, the vinegar, fish sauce, ginger and more salt and pepper in
a screw-top jar and shake to combine. Place the mixed leaves, bok choy, radishes
and cooled mushrooms in a bowl and toss with enough of the dressing to coat well.
Serve immediately.

45

SUPERSLAW

Serves: 4 people as a side • *Time: 10 minutes, plus 20 minutes infusing*

CONTAINS
Vitamins A, C, K & biotin (B7), copper, manganese,
calcium, flavonoids and other phytochemicals,
potassium, carotenoids, fibre

YOU NEED
2 tablespoons natural yoghurt • 2 tablespoons **tahini**

1 tablespoon **lemon juice**, plus extra to taste • ½ garlic clove, finely chopped

sea salt flakes • freshly ground black pepper

½ medium **turnip**, about 100g, peeled • 175g **swede**, peeled

1 medium **carrot**, peeled • 1 red apple • 1 small handful **coriander**, chopped

46

For the dressing, place the yoghurt, tahini, lemon juice, garlic and salt and pepper
in a screw-top jar, add 2 tablespoons water and shake vigorously to combine. Set
aside. For the salad, cut the vegetables and apple into fine matchsticks – ideally,
finely slice on a mandoline, then cut into thin strips. Place in a salad bowl and add
the coriander. Pour over the dressing and toss to coat. Add more lemon juice and
salt and pepper to taste. Set aside for up to 20 minutes before serving to let
the flavours infuse.

GOODNESS BOWL

Serves: 1 • Time: 20 minutes

CONTAINS
Vitamins A, B-group C & K, manganese, copper,
glucosinolates, flavonoids and other phytochemicals,
calcium, magnesium

YOU NEED
70g red quinoa, rinsed and drained • 1 egg

a large mixed handful of **kale, mustard leaves** and **beet greens** , finely sliced

1 spring onion, finely sliced • ½ green jalapeño

1 tablespoon chopped **coriander** • 2 tablespoons extra virgin olive oil

2 tablespoons **lime juice** • ½ garlic clove, crushed • sea salt flakes • freshly

ground black pepper • 2 tablespoons toasted **peanuts**, roughly chopped

Cook the quinoa according to the packet instructions. Drain (if necessary) and set aside. Bring a small pan of water to the boil, lower in the egg and cook for 6 minutes. Transfer to cold water, then peel and leave whole. Steam the mixed vegetables until just tender. Place all the remaining ingredients except the peanuts in a screw-top jar and shake to combine. To serve, place the quinoa in a bowl and top with the steamed vegetables. Halve the egg and add to the bowl. Spoon over the dressing, scatter with the peanuts and serve immediately.

ZINGY CHEAT'S PIZZA

Serves: 1 • Time: 15 minutes

CONTAINS

Vitamins A, B-group, C & K, flavonoids, carotenoids,
folate, manganese, fibre

YOU NEED

½ x 400g can chopped **tomatoes** • sea salt flakes • freshly ground black pepper

1 large tortilla • a handful of **baby spinach**, sliced

4 **artichoke hearts** in oil, drained and quartered

peel from ½ **preserved lemon**, finely sliced • 1 mozzarella ball, about 125g, sliced

olive oil, for drizzling • **basil leaves**, for sprinkling

Tip the tomatoes into a small pan, season with salt and pepper, stir and simmer
until thickened. Set aside. Place the tortilla in a hot frying pan until it starts to puff
up and turn brown underneath. Transfer to a baking sheet and spread the tomato
sauce over the top. Arrange the spinach, artichokes and preserved lemon peel on
top, and season with salt and pepper. Top with the mozzarella slices and drizzle with
olive oil. Place under a hot grill until the cheese melts and turns golden.
Serve sprinkled with basil leaves. Cut into slices to serve.

TOFU BITES & PUNCHY PICKLES

Serves: 2–4 people as a side • Time: 30 minutes

CONTAINS
Vitamins A, C, K & biotin (B7), carotenoids, flavonoids,
protein, iron, magnesium & calcium

YOU NEED

1 large **carrot**, cut into fine matchsticks • 1 teaspoon caster sugar

¼ teaspoon fine sea salt • 4 tablespoons rice vinegar

1 tablespoon soy sauce • 1½ tablespoons **lime juice**

½ tablespoon dashi or vegetable stock • 100g cornflour

sea salt flakes • freshly ground black pepper

350g **silken tofu**, cut into 2cm squares • vegetable oil, for shallow frying

Toss together the carrot, sugar, fine sea salt and half the vinegar. Set aside for
30 minutes, then drain. Meanwhile, whisk together the remaining vinegar, the
soy, lime juice and stock in a small bowl and set aside. Place the cornflour on a
shallow plate and season with salt and pepper. Roll the tofu in the flour to coat.
Heat enough oil in a frying pan to come 5mm up the sides and fry the tofu, turning
constantly, for 5 minutes, until crisp and golden all over. Serve immediately, with the
pickled carrots and sauce alongside for dipping.

SUNSHINE SOUP

Serves: 4 people • Time: 50 minutes, plus 5 minutes cooling

CONTAINS
Vitamins A, B-group & C, flavonoids, carotenoids,
copper, manganese, calcium

YOU NEED

2 **red, yellow** or **orange peppers**, halved and deseeded

500g **tomatoes**, halved • 2 tablespoons olive oil, plus extra for drizzling

a pinch of saffron threads, chopped • 1 litre hot chicken or vegetable stock

1 red onion, chopped • 2 garlic cloves, finely sliced

1 heaped teaspoon chopped oregano • sea salt flakes

freshly ground black pepper • natural yoghurt or crème fraîche, to serve

sesame seeds, toasted, to serve

Place the peppers and tomatoes in a baking tray cut-side down, drizzle with olive oil
and place under a hot grill until the peppers blacken and the tomatoes blister. Cool
down, then peel off the pepper skins. Add the saffron to the stock and set aside.
Heat the olive oil in a pan and fry the onion for 8 minutes until soft. Add the garlic
and fry for a few minutes. Add the grilled peppers and tomatoes, stock and oregano.
Season with salt and pepper and simmer for 20 minutes. Cool slightly then blitz in
a food processor or with a blender. Warm through. Serve with a swirl of yoghurt or
crème fraîche and sesame seeds.

SOUP SOOTHER

Serves: 4 people • Time: 20 minutes

CONTAINS

Vitamins A, C & K, potassium, glucosinolates, copper,
magnesium, iodine, minerals, phytochemicals, calcium,
protein & iron

YOU NEED

500ml vegetable or chicken stock • ½ tablespoon soy sauce

1 teaspoon dried **wakame** • 80g **firm tofu**, cubed

1 head of **bok choy**, about 100g, leaves trimmed and separated

Place the stock in a pan, add the soy. Bring to the boil then set aside for 10 minutes. Meanwhile, soak the wakame in hot water for 10 minutes then drain and cut away any tough spines. Add the wakame, tofu and bok choy to the bowl. Pour the stock into the bowl and serve immediately.

CREAMY COMFORT SOUP

Serves: 4 people • *Time: 30 minutes, plus 5 minutes cooling*

CONTAINS

Vitamins C & K, folate, molybdenum & fibre

YOU NEED

1 red onion, chopped • 1 teaspoon ground cumin

300g **cauliflower**, cut into florets and stalks chopped • 1 litre vegetable stock

240g cooked or canned **red kidney** or **pinto beans**, drained and rinsed

crème fraîche, to serve

Heat the oil in a pan and cook the onion for about 8 minutes. Add the cumin and
the cauliflower and cook over a medium-high heat, stirring, until the cauliflower
starts to brown. Add the stock and beans. Reduce the heat and simmer uncovered
until the cauliflower is tender. When the cauliflower is cooked, cool slightly then
carefully blitz the soup with a food processor or hand blender. Warm through over a
medium heat, add salt and pepper to taste and top with crème fraîche
before serving.

PEANUT HUMMUS

Serves: 2–4 people as a side • *Time: 5 minutes*

CONTAINS
Vitamins B-group & C, copper, manganese, flavonoids

YOU NEED

1 x 400g can chickpeas • 1 small garlic clove • 3 tablespoons smooth
peanut butter • 3 tablespoons **lemon juice**, plus extra to taste
1½ teaspoons ground cumin • sea salt flakes • freshly ground black pepper
olive oil, for drizzling • your choice of chopped vegetables, to serve

Drain the chickpeas, reserving the liquid, and rinse. Combine the garlic, peanut
butter, lemon juice and cumin in a food processor and blitz until smooth. Add
some of the reserved chickpea liquid to loosen if too thick, and adjust the seasoning
according to taste with extra lemon juice and salt and pepper. Transfer to a shallow
bowl and drizzle with olive oil. Serve with your choice of chopped
vegetables for dipping.

VITABOOST FRITTATA

Serves: 4-6 people • Time: 45 minutes

CONTAINS

Vitamin A, B6, C & K, carotenoids, magnesium,
flavonoids, molybdenum, folate and fibre

YOU NEED

300g **acorn squash**, peeled, deseeded and diced small • 4 tablespoons olive oil

sea salt flakes • freshly ground black pepper

150g **Swiss chard**, sliced • 4 eggs, lightly beaten

200g cooked **black, green** or **Puy lentils** • 100g feta cheese, crumbled

Preheat the oven to 200°C/400°F/Gas 6. Place the squash in a baking tray, toss
with 1 tablespoon of oil and season. Roast for 30 minutes, or until tender.
Heat 1 tablespoon of oil in a 20cm frying pan and fry the Swiss chard with salt
and pepper. Transfer to a bowl, leave to cool slightly, then stir in the remaining
ingredients including the squash. Wipe out the frying pan, heat the remaining
oil and pour in the egg mixture. Cook over a medium–high heat until golden
underneath, then place under a hot grill until set. Invert onto a plate to serve.

SIDE PLATES

Just because sides are the supporting role in a meal doesn't mean they can't be packed with nutrients – quite the opposite. In fact, all these sides are so loaded with flavour and goodness you could enjoy them as stand-alone meals. Eating your greens has never been easier.

Power plate • Spicy stir-fried greens • Green
smash • Nutty griddled lettuce • Glowing greens
Creamy turnip bake • Healing curry bowl
Mediterranean vegetable bowl • Ultimate
lentil braise • Supercharged carrots
Powerhouse tomatoes • Warm garden salad
Hearty spiced stew

POWER PLATE

Serves: 4 people as a side • *Time: 40 minutes*

CONTAINS

Vitamin A, B-group, C & K, copper, manganese, fibre,
carotenoids, calcium, magnesium, flavonoids and
other phytochemicals

YOU NEED

800g **acorn squash**, cut into wedges 2cm at the widest part

3 tablespoons olive oil, plus extra for drizzling • sea salt flakes

freshly ground black pepper • 160g vacuum-packed **chestnuts**, halved

6 tablespoons Greek-style yoghurt • 1 tablespoon Sriracha sauce, or more
to taste • 2 large handfuls of **beet greens**, chopped

1 large handful of **coriander**, chopped

Heat the oven to 200°C/400°F/Gas 6. Place the squash in a baking tray, toss with the olive oil and season. Roast for 30 minutes until almost tender. Add the chestnuts to the pan, turn to coat in the oil and return to the oven for a further 10 minutes. To make the dressing, stir together the yoghurt and Sriracha. To serve, scatter the beet greens over a serving platter, drizzle with olive oil and toss to coat. Arrange the roasted squash and chestnuts on top, then pour over the yoghurt dressing. Serve scattered with the coriander.

67

SPICY STIR-FRIED GREENS

Serves: 4 people as a side • *Time: 10 minutes*

CONTAINS

Vitamins A, C & K, flavonoids and other
phytochemicals, potassium, glucosinolates, copper,
manganese, calcium

YOU NEED

2 tablespoons groundnut or flavourless oil • 3cm piece peeled fresh ginger,
finely chopped • a small handful of **coriander** stalks, finely chopped
1 red chilli, or more to taste, deseeded and finely sliced
4 large heads of **bok choy,** quartered lengthways • 2 tablespoons mirin
120ml chicken or vegetable stock • a splash of soy sauce, or more to taste
sesame oil, for drizzling

Heat the oil in a frying pan or wok over a high heat. Add the ginger, coriander stalks and chilli, and stir-fry for 1 minute. Add the bok choy and cook until starting to soften, then add the mirin, stock and soy. Cook until the bok choy is tender but still retains some bite. Transfer to a serving bowl and drizzle with sesame oil. Serve immediately.

GREEN SMASH

Serves: 4 people as a side • *Time: 30 minutes*

CONTAINS

Vitamins A, B6, C & K, manganese, glucosinolates,
flavonoids, omega-3 fatty acids, fibre, protein, iron,
magnesium & calcium

YOU NEED

600g floury potatoes, cut into chunks with the skins left on
2 tablespoons unsalted butter • 60g **kale**, finely sliced • 60g **collard greens**
or **spring greens**, finely sliced • 60g **cabbage**, finely sliced • 200ml **flax, soya** or
dairy milk, plus extra if needed • 1 garlic clove, bruised • sea salt flakes
freshly ground black pepper

POTENTIAL
BENEFITS

protects against *cancer &*
cardiovascular problems
• **lowers** *cholesterol*
• **supports** *digestive & bone*
health • **eases** *post-menopausal*
symptoms• *anti-inflammatory*

Steam the potatoes until tender. Melt half the butter in a large frying pan and add
the kale, collard greens and cabbage. Stir-fry until tender but retaining some bite.
Set aside. Place the milk in a pan with the garlic, bring to the boil, then remove
from the heat and keep warm. When the potatoes are cooked, mash with the
remaining butter and milk, discarding the garlic, until smooth and creamy. Add
more milk to achieve the desired consistency if necessary. Mix in the vegetables and
add salt and pepper to taste. Serve immediately.

NUTTY GRIDDLED LETTUCE

Serves: 4 people as a side • *Time: 15 minutes*

CONTAINS

Vitamins A, B-group, E & K, folate, flavonoids,
carotenoids, manganese, copper, fibre

YOU NEED

2 tablespoons mayonnaise • 2 tablespoons crème fraîche

½ garlic clove, crushed • 5 **basil leaves**, finely sliced

sea salt flakes • freshly ground black pepper

3 large **romaine lettuce**, halved lengthways • olive oil, for brushing

3 hard-boiled eggs, chopped • 3 tablespoons **toasted hazelnuts**, chopped

POTENTIAL
BENEFITS

protects against
*cardiovascular disease
& cancer*
• **lowers** *cholesterol*
• **regulates** *blood sugar*
• **supports** *skin health*
• *antibacterial*

For the dressing, place the mayonnaise, crème fraîche, garlic, basil, salt and pepper
and a splash of water in a screw-top jar and shake vigorously. Add more water to
loosen if needed. Set aside. Heat a griddle pan over a high heat. Brush the cut-side
of the lettuce with olive oil and griddle cut-side down until charred and slightly
wilted. Flip and briefly cook the other side – the lettuce should still be firm at the
centre. Transfer to a serving plate, drizzle with dressing and top with egg. Drizzle
over more dressing and scatter with the hazelnuts to serve.

GLOWING GREENS

Serves: 4 people as a side • Time: 10 minutes

CONTAINS

Vitamins A, B-group, C, E & K, manganese,
glucosinolates, flavonoids, folate, copper, fibre

YOU NEED

300g mixed leafy vegetables such as **collard greens** or **spring greens**,
kale and **chicory**, sliced • 2 tablespoons **hazelnut oil**
4 tablespoons balsamic vinegar • 80g unsalted butter • sea salt flakes
freshly ground black pepper

Steam the leafy vegetables for about 2 minutes until just tender. Transfer to a serving bowl, toss with the hazelnut oil and set aside somewhere warm. Place the balsamic vinegar in a small pan and cook over a medium heat. Stir constantly while the mixture bubbles and thickens, until it has reduced to a syrup. Add the butter and cook until melted into the syrup. Pour the syrup over the greens, toss and season generously with salt and pepper. Serve immediately.

CREAMY TURNIP BAKE

Serves: 4 people • *Time: 50 minutes*

CONTAINS

Vitamins A, C & K, folate, calcium, flavonoids,
omega-3 fatty acids, fibre, protein, iron, magnesium,
carotenoids, manganese, glucosinolates

YOU NEED

400ml **flax, soya** or dairy milk, plus extra if needed • 400ml double cream

2 garlic cloves, minced • 2 thyme sprigs

2 bay leaves • sea salt flakes • freshly ground black pepper

600g **turnips**, peeled and finely sliced, ideally on a mandoline

a large handful of **turnip greens** (**baby kale** or **spinach** also work well), sliced

90g Gruyère cheese, grated

Preheat the oven to 200°C/400°F/Gas 6. Put the milk, cream, garlic, thyme and
bay leaves in a pan and season. Simmer gently for 3 minutes, then remove from
the heat. Add the turnips, top up with milk to cover if necessary, then simmer until
just tender. Lightly steam the turnip greens until almost tender. Drain the turnips,
reserve the creamy milk and remove the thyme and bay leaves. Layer the turnips,
turnip greens and cheese in a baking dish, pouring creamy milk over each layer.
Top with cheese. Bake for 30 minutes, or until golden and bubbling.

HEALING CURRY BOWL

Serves: 4 people as a side • *Time: 40 minutes*

CONTAINS
Vitamins A, B6 & C, fibre, carotenoids, potassium

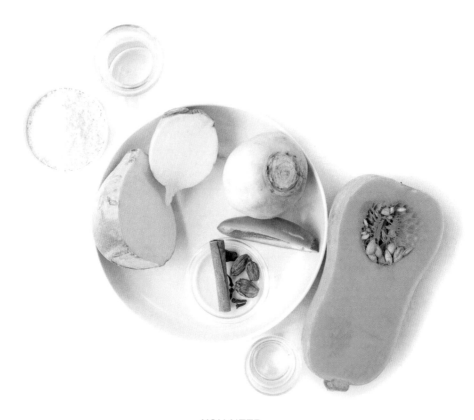

YOU NEED
25g desiccated coconut • 125ml boiling water

3 tablespoons vegetable oil • 4 cardamom pods • 4 cloves

1 medium green chilli, sliced in half lengthways and deseeded

½ cinnamon stick • 500g **squash**, peeled, seeded and cut into 2.5cm pieces

250g **swede**, peeled and cut into 2.5cm pieces

250g **turnips**, peeled and cut into 2.5cm pieces

¼ teaspoon sea salt flakes

Soak the coconut in the boiling water and set aside. Heat the oil in a large pan until
very hot, then add the cardamom pods, cloves, chilli and cinnamon stick. Fry for
30 seconds, stirring constantly, then add the vegetables. Cook, stirring, until golden
(about 8 minutes). Reduce the heat to low, add the salt and cook, covered, until the
vegetables are very tender (about 20 minutes). Stir often to ensure they don't stick.
Add the coconut and soaking water. Stir to coat and cook for a few minutes more
until the water has evaporated before serving.

MEDITERRANEAN VEGETABLE BOWL

Serves: 4 people as a side • *Time: 40 minutes*

CONTAINS
Vitamin A, B-group, C & K, flavonoids, carotenoids,
folate, fibre

YOU NEED
300g aubergines, cut into large cubes • 1 teaspoon fine sea salt

120ml olive oil • 1 red onion, thinly sliced • 2 garlic cloves, finely chopped

2 large ripe **tomatoes**, diced • ½ **red pepper**, diced

140g **artichoke hearts** in oil (drained weight), cut into bite-sized pieces

1 heaped tablespoon capers • 30g golden sultanas

a generous pinch of chilli flakes • 2 tablespoons red wine vinegar

sea salt flakes • freshly ground black pepper • a handful of **basil**, torn

POTENTIAL
BENEFITS

protects against
cardiovascular disease & cancer
• **lowers** *cholesterol*
• **regulates** *blood sugar*
• **supports** *bone & digestive
health & weight loss*
• *anti-inflammatory,
antibacterial*

Place the aubergines in a colander set over a bowl, sprinkle with salt and drain for 20 minutes, then pat dry with kitchen paper. Heat 2 tablespoons of oil in a frying pan and fry the onion until soft. Add the garlic and fry for 2 minutes. Transfer to a plate. Wipe out the pan, heat the remaining oil over a medium–high heat and fry the aubergine until golden. Return the onion and garlic and add the tomatoes, pepper and 120ml water. Simmer for 15 minutes. Take off the heat and add the remaining ingredients. Season and sprinkle with basil.

ULTIMATE LENTIL BRAISE

Serves: 4 people • *Time: 45 minutes*

CONTAINS

Vitamin B-group & C, flavonoids, carotenoids,
molybdenum, folate, fibre

YOU NEED

2 tablespoons olive oil • 2 onions, chopped

3 garlic cloves, finely chopped • 250g **Puy lentils**, rinsed and drained

1 x 400g can chopped **tomatoes** • 600ml vegetable stock

Heat the oil in an ovenproof pan, add the onions and cook over a medium heat for
5 minutes until they start to soften. Add the garlic and a splash of water then reduce
the heat and cover. Cook for 10 minutes, or until soft, adding more water if needed.
Add the lentils and simmer for a few minutes more. Add the tomatoes and stock,
cover and cook for 20–30 minutes.

SUPERCHARGED CARROTS

Serves 4 people as a side • Time: 30 minutes

CONTAINS

Vitamins A, C, K & biotin (B7), carotenoids, copper,
flavonoids, manganese, calcium

YOU NEED

1 large bunch of **carrots** with the green tops on • 2 tablespoons olive oil
sea salt flakes • freshly ground black pepper • 90ml extra virgin olive oil
30ml **lemon juice** • 1 garlic clove, crushed • 2 tablespoons runny honey
¼ teaspoon wholegrain mustard • 1 tablespoon **black sesame seeds**

Set the oven to 200°C/400°F/Gas 6. Cut the green tops off the carrots, roughly chop and set aside. In a baking tray, toss the carrots with the 2 tablespoons olive oil and season. Roast for 25–30 minutes, or until tender and starting to caramelise. For the dressing, place the oil, lemon, garlic, honey, mustard and salt and pepper in a food processor and blitz. Add the carrot tops and briefly blitz again. When the carrots are cooked, toss with enough of the dressing to coat and sprinkle with sesame seeds. Serve with the rest of the dressing on the side.

POWERHOUSE TOMATOES

Serves 4 people as a side • *Time: 1½ hours*

CONTAINS
Vitamins B-group, C & K, flavonoids, carotenoids

YOU NEED

6 medium **tomatoes**, halved • 3 garlic cloves, crushed • a large handful of **basil**

3 tablespoons olive oil • sea salt flakes • freshly ground black pepper

Preheat the oven to 170°C/325°F/Gas 3. Place the tomatoes in a baking tray.
Mix all the other ingredients together in a screw-top jar then pour the mixture over
the tomatoes and toss them in it. Arrange in the tray cut-side down and roast for
1–1½ hours, depending on ripeness and size. They should be very soft and wrinkled
when done. Serve hot or cold.

WARM GARDEN SALAD

Serves 4 people as a side • Time: 40 minutes

CONTAINS

Vitamin A, C & K, carotenoids, folate, flavonoids

YOU NEED

2 bunches breakfast **radishes** with tops on

6 red or green **chicory heads**, halved lengthways • 90ml tablespoons

unsalted butter, melted • 2 tablespoons olive oil • 2 tablespoon runny honey

a generous squeeze of **lemon juice** • 1 sprig thyme, leaves removed

sea salt flakes • freshly ground black pepper

Preheat the oven to 190°C/375°F/Gas 5. Cut the tops off the radishes, trim the
leaves and set aside. Halve or quarter the radishes so they are roughly the same size
and place in a baking tray with the chicory halves. Whisk together the butter, olive
oil, honey, lemon juice, thyme and salt and pepper. Pour over the vegetables and
toss. Roast for 25–30 minutes until tender, shaking the pan once or twice during
cooking. As soon as the vegetables are cooked, add the radish leaves to the hot pan
and toss until wilted. Season to taste then serve.

HEARTY SPICED STEW

Serves: 2 people • Time: 1 hour plus 30 minutes draining

CONTAINS
Vitamins A, B-group & C, flavonoids, carotenoids

YOU NEED

200g aubergine, cut into 2cm cubes • ½ teaspoon fine sea salt

2 tablespoons olive oil • 3 garlic cloves, chopped • ½ red onion, chopped

150g ripe **tomatoes**, chopped • 1 green chilli, finely chopped

½ teaspoon garam masala • 150g **red pepper**, chopped into 2cm chunks

sea salt flakes • freshly ground black pepper

Preheat the oven to 220°C/425°F/Gas 7. Place the aubergine in a colander set over
a bowl, toss with the salt and drain for 30 minutes. Pat dry, place in a baking tray
lined with baking paper and toss with half the oil. Roast for 15 minutes, or until
tender. Heat the remaining oil in a frying pan and fry the garlic and onion until
golden. Add the tomatoes, chilli and garam masala and cook for 2 minutes.
Stir in the pepper, aubergine, 50ml water and salt and pepper. Cover and cook for
30 minutes, or until tender, adding more water if it dries out.

BIG PLATES

Anyone who believes that highly nutritious main meals must, by definition, be dull and boring should think again. These vibrant plates are absolutely delicious — and also happen to be incredibly beneficial for your health and wellbeing.

Glowing green pesto pasta • Nourishing noodle bowl • Cauliflower risotto • Detox bowl Green pasta bake • Cosy root vegetable salad Kale & bean hash • Bean & chocolate chilli Roasted mackerel & salsa • Mackerel & supersauce toast • Salmon with watercress sauce Salmon burger • Cheesy vegetable pie

GLOWING GREEN PESTO PASTA

Serves: 1 person • Time: 15 minutes

CONTAINS
Vitamins A, B-group, C & K, manganese,
glucosinolates, flavonoids, copper, manganese,

YOU NEED

100g fusilli pasta • 2 tablespoons extra virgin olive oil, plus extra if needed
and for tossing • 20g **kale**, tough stalks removed and chopped • ½ garlic clove
5g **basil** leaves • 10g unsalted **roasted peanuts**, roughly chopped, plus extra
for sprinkling • 15g Parmesan cheese, grated, plus extra for sprinkling
lemon juice, to taste • sea salt flakes • freshly ground black pepper

POTENTIAL
BENEFITS

protects against *heart
disease, stroke, cancer,
rheumatoid arthritis, cell damage
& Alzheimer's disease* • **lowers**
cholesterol • **regulates** *blood
sugar* • **supports** *the immune
system* • *anti-inflammatory,
antibacterial*

Cook the pasta according to the packet instructions. Drain and toss with a little olive
oil. Meanwhile, scrunch the kale with your hands to soften, place in a mini food
processor or mortar and pulse or pound to a rough paste. Add the garlic, the
2 tablespoons olive oil, the basil, peanuts and Parmesan. Blitz or pound to the
desired consistency, adding more oil if necessary. Add lemon juice and salt and
pepper to taste, then toss through the hot pasta. Serve sprinkled with Parmesan
and chopped peanuts.

NOURISHING NOODLE BOWL

Serves: 1 person • *Time: 25 minutes*

CONTAINS

Vitamin A, B-group, C, D & K, selenium, omega-3 fatty
acids, potassium, glucosinolates

YOU NEED

1 skinless **salmon fillet**, about 120g • 3 tablespoons soy sauce
100g medium-width flat rice noodles • 2 tablespoons groundnut
or any other flavourless olive oil, plus extra for tossing • 1 small bunch
bok choy, leaves separated • a pinch of chilli flakes, or to taste

Place the salmon in a shallow bowl, pour over half the soy and turn to coat.
Set aside. Meanwhile, soak the noodles in boiling water for 5 minutes, then rinse
and toss with a splash of oil. Set aside. Heat half the oil in a frying pan and fry the
salmon for 2–3 minutes each side, or until just cooked through. Flake the fish and
set aside. Wipe out the pan, add the remaining oil and stir-fry the bok choy for
1 minute. Add the noodles, chilli flakes, salmon and remaining soy and gently toss.
Serve immediately.

CAULIFLOWER RISOTTO

Serves: 1 person • Time: 20 minutes

CONTAINS

Vitamins C & K, folate, protein, iron, magnesium,
calcium, fibre, flavonoids

YOU NEED

300g **cauliflower**, broken into small florets • 1 heaped teaspoon **white
miso paste** • 1½ tablespoons unsalted butter • ½ tablespoon olive oil • 1 shallot,
finely chopped • 70g **artichokes** in oil (drained weight), cut into bite-size
pieces • 3 heaped tablespoons finely grated Parmesan, plus extra to serve
finely grated zest of ½ **lemon** • sea salt flakes
freshly ground black pepper • a handful of **basil leaves**, sliced

Blitz the cauliflower in a food processor to the size of rice grains. Dissolve the miso
paste in 300ml boiling water. Heat 1 tablespoon of the butter and the oil in a pan,
add the shallot and gently cook for 5 minutes until soft. Add the cauliflower and
stir to coat. Add half the miso stock and simmer for 10 minutes, stirring and adding
a bit more stock now and then. The cauliflower should be tender but retain some
bite, with enough liquid to make a sauce. Fold in the artichokes, remove from the
heat and add the remaining butter, the Parmesan, lemon zest and salt and pepper.
Serve sprinkled with basil leaves and Parmesan.

DETOX BOWL

Serves: 1 person • Time: 40 minutes

CONTAINS

Vitamin A, B-group, C & E, fibre, carotenoids, flavonoids
and other phytochemicals, manganese, copper, fibre

YOU NEED

300g **acorn squash**, peeled, deseeded and cut into bite-size chunks

4 tablespoons olive oil, plus extra for drizzling • sea salt flakes

freshly ground black pepper • 160g giant (Israeli) couscous

375ml chicken or vegetable stock • 1 tablespoon **lemon juice**

1 teaspoon Dijon mustard • a handful of rocket

a handful of **dried cranberries** • a handful of **pecan nuts**, chopped

Preheat the oven to 200°C/400°F/Gas 6. Place the squash in a baking tray, drizzle with olive oil and season. Roast for 20–30 minutes, or until tender and slightly caramelised. Place the couscous in a pan, add 1 tablespoon of oil and stir over a medium–high heat until toasted. Add the stock, bring to the boil, then reduce the heat to low and cover. Cook for 15 minutes, or until the stock is absorbed. Whisk together the remaining oil, lemon, mustard and salt and pepper. When the couscous is cooked, remove from the heat, add the rocket and stir through until wilted. Add the dressing, cranberries, pecans and squash.

GREEN PASTA BAKE

Serves: 1 person • *Time: 1 hour*

CONTAINS
Vitamins A, B-group, C, E & K, manganese, folate,
calcium, flavonoids, magnesium, glucosinolates, copper,
carotenoids, selenium, fibre

YOU NEED

85g penne pasta • 20g unsalted butter, plus more for greasing
15g plain flour • 250ml milk, plus extra if needed
40g Comte, Gruyère or Cheddar cheese, grated • ¼ teaspoon paprika
a pinch of nutmeg • ½ teaspoon Dijon mustard • sea salt flakes
freshly ground black pepper • 50g **greens** such as **collard greens,
beet greens, turnip greens, kale, spinach** or **spring greens**, finely sliced
25g sourdough or country-style bread, torn • 2 teaspoons olive oil
2 teaspoons **sunflower seeds** • 2 teaspoons **ground hazelnuts**

Cook the penne in salted boiling water according to the packet instructions. Drain
and set aside. Preheat the oven to 180°C/350°F/Gas 4 and lightly butter a small
gratin dish. Melt the butter in a pan until foaming then add the flour. Stir constantly
over a medium heat for 1 minute then gradually whisk in the milk. Gently cook for
5 minutes until starting to thicken, then stir in the cheeses, seasonings, vegetables
and pasta. Tip into the dish. Blitz the bread, oil, sunflower seeds and hazelnuts in
a mini food processor until the mixture resembles breadcrumbs. Spread over the
pasta and bake for 30 minutes.

COSY ROOT VEGETABLE SALAD

Serves: 1 person • Time: 50 minutes

CONTAINS
Vitamins A, B-group, C & K, carotenoids, flavonoids

YOU NEED

2 medium **carrots**, cut lengthways and crossways

80g **turnips**, peeled and cut into 7x2cm batons

3 tablespoons olive oil • 2 tablespoons **lemon juice** • sea salt flakes

freshly ground black pepper • 50g **cherry tomatoes**, quartered

150g cooked wheat berries or farro • 60g feta cheese, crumbled

Preheat the oven to 200°C/400°F/Gas 6. Place the carrots and turnips in a baking tray. Toss with the 1 tablespoon of the olive oil, half the lemon juice and salt and pepper. Bake for 20 minutes, add the tomato, toss to coat in the pan juices and roast for a further 20 minutes, or until tender. Toss the wheat berries or farro, feta cheese and the roasted vegetables with the remaining olive oil and lemon juice and add salt and pepper to taste. Serve immediately.

KALE & BEAN HASH

Serves: 1 person • *Time: 20 minutes*

CONTAINS
Vitamins A, B-group, C, E & K, manganese,
glucosinolates, flavonoids, copper, fibre, selenium

YOU NEED

40g **curly kale**, thick stalks removed and finely sliced

1 tablespoon olive oil, plus extra if needed • ½ garlic clove, finely chopped

1 heaped tablespoon coarse breadcrumbs, ideally from a rye or sourdough loaf

1 tablespoons **hazelnuts**, finely chopped • 1 tablespoon **sunflower seeds**

grated zest and juice of ½ **lemon** • a pinch of chilli flakes

3 tablespoons parsley, chopped • sea salt flakes • freshly ground black pepper

100g cooked or canned gigantes (or giant) beans, drained and rinsed

3 tablespoons finely grated Parmesan

Steam the kale until tender. Set aside. To make the sprinkle, heat half the oil in a
frying pan and briefly fry the garlic until pale gold. Add the breadcrumbs, hazelnuts
and sunflower seeds, and stir-fry over a medium–high heat until crisp. Stir in the
lemon zest, chilli flakes, parsley and salt and pepper. Set aside. Wipe out the pan,
add the remaining olive oil and fry the beans in a single layer for a couple of
minutes until golden underneath, then flip and cook the other side. Add the kale,
gently toss and stir in the lemon juice. Generously season. Serve the beans and kale
topped with the sprinkle and Parmesan.

BEAN & CHOCOLATE CHILLI

Serves: 1 person • Time: 40 minutes

CONTAINS

Vitamins B-group & C, flavonoids, carotenoids,
molybdenum, folate and fibre, minerals, flavonoids

YOU NEED

1 tablespoon olive oil • ½ red onion, chopped • 1 small garlic clove, chopped
½ small red chilli, finely sliced • 100ml **passata** • 80ml vegetable stock, plus
extra if needed • 200g canned **red kidney beans**, rinsed and drained
10g **dark chocolate**, 100% cocoa solids, shaved • ½ teaspoon ground cumin
sea salt flakes • freshly ground black pepper • a squeeze of lime

Heat the oil in a small pan and gently fry the onion for 8 minutes until soft. Add the garlic and chilli, and cook for a few minutes more. Add the passata, stock, beans, chocolate, cumin and salt and pepper. Bring to the boil, reduce the heat and gently simmer uncovered for 20 minutes, stirring regularly. Add the squeeze of lime and more salt and pepper to taste. This dish is delicious served with steamed rice.

ROASTED MACKEREL & SALSA

Serves: 1 person • Time: 20 minutes

CONTAINS
Vitamins B-group, C, D & K, omega-3 fatty acids,
flavonoids and other phytochemicals, carotenoids

YOU NEED
1 whole **mackerel**, cleaned and gutted • 2 slices of **lemon**, plus the juice of ½
lemon • 2 tablespoons olive oil, plus extra for drizzling • sea salt flakes
freshly ground black pepper • 5 **cherry tomatoes**, 3 halved and 2 diced
½ garlic clove, finely chopped • 1 tablespoon chopped **coriander**

POTENTIAL
BENEFITS

protects against
*cancer, rheumatoid arthritis,
cardiovascular disease & cell
damage* • **lowers** *cholesterol*
• **regulates** *blood sugar & pressure*
• **supports** *the immune system,
bone health & weight loss*
• *anti-inflammatory,
antibacterial*

Preheat the oven to 180°C/350°F/Gas 4. Cut 3 slashes in both sides of the mackerel.
Stuff the inside with the lemon and season inside and out. Place in a small baking
tray and pour over the lemon juice. Arrange the tomatoes around the fish and
drizzle with olive oil. Bake for 15 minutes, or until the fish flesh comes away from
the bone easily. Gently heat the olive oil in a small pan, add the garlic and gently
cook. Add the diced tomatoes and coriander and warm through. Serve the fish with
the sauce spooned over and tomatoes alongside.

MACKEREL & SUPERSAUCE TOAST

Serves: 1 person • *Time: 20 minutes*

CONTAINS
Vitamins B-group, C & D, omega-3 fatty acids,
flavonoids, carotenoids

YOU NEED
1 **mackerel** fillet • 1 tablespoon olive oil, plus extra for brushing
½ teaspoon fine sea salt • ½ red onion, finely chopped
½ tablespoon balsamic vinegar • 100ml **passata** • ¼ teaspoon smoked paprika
sea salt flakes • freshly ground black pepper • 1 slice soughdough bread

POTENTIAL
BENEFITS

protects against
cardiovascular disease & cancer
• **lowers** *cholesterol*
• **regulates** *blood pressure*
• **supports** *bone health
& weight loss*
• *anti-inflammatory*

Brush both sides of the mackerel with oil and sprinkle with salt. Heat the oil in
a small pan, add the onion and cook until soft. Add the vinegar and cook until
reduced to a syrup. Stir in the passata, paprika, 50ml water and salt and pepper.
Gently simmer until reduced to a thick sauce, then remove from the heat. Put the
mackerel on a foil-lined grill tray skin-side up and cook under a hot grill for
2 minutes, or until the skin bubbles. Flip and grill for 1 minute. Toast the bread.
To serve, place the mackerel on the toast with the sauce spooned over.

SALMON WITH WATERCRESS SAUCE

Serves: 1 person • Time: 20 minutes

CONTAINS

Vitamins A, B-group, C, D & K, selenium, omega-3
fatty acids, flavonoids

YOU NEED

1 **salmon fillet**, about 120g • a squeeze of **lemon** • sea salt flakes

freshly ground black pepper • 1 tablespoon unsalted butter

1 shallot, finely chopped • 70g **watercress**

120ml chicken, fish or vegetable stock • 1 tablespoon crème fraîche

Preheat the oven to 180°C/350°F/Gas 4. Place the salmon in a baking tray, squeeze
over the lemon and season. Cover tightly with foil and roast for 15 minutes. Melt
the butter in a pan and fry the shallot until soft. Chop half the watercress (including
stalks) and add. Stir-fry for 2 minutes, then add the stock. Cook for 1 minute, stir
in the crème fraîche and season. Cool slightly, blitz in a blender until smooth,
then pass through a sieve if desired. Add salt and pepper to taste before warming
through. Remove the tough stalks from the remaining watercress and place the
leaves on a plate. Top with the salmon and sauce.

SALMON BURGER

Serves: 1 person • Time: 25 minutes, plus 20 minutes chilling

CONTAINS
Vitamins A, B-group, C, D & K, folate, carotenoids,
selenium, omega-3 fatty acids

YOU NEED

1 skinless **salmon fillet**, about 120g, cut into pieces

½ teaspoon fresh ginger, grated • ½ garlic clove, finely chopped

10g fresh breadcrumbs • sea salt flakes • freshly ground black pepper

plain flour, for dusting • 2 tablespoons rapeseed or groundnut oil

1 burger bun, 1 tablespoon mayonnaise and a handful of **rocket**, to serve

Pulse the salmon in a food processor until roughly chopped. Transfer to a bowl and mix through the ginger, garlic, breadcrumbs and salt and pepper. Shape into a patty and chill for 20 minutes. Then lightly dust the salmon patty with flour. Heat the oil in a frying pan and fry the patty for 3–4 minutes each side. Serve in a burger bun on top of mayonnaise and rocket.

CHEESY VEGETABLE PIE

Serves: 1 person • Time: 1 hour

CONTAINS

Vitamins A, C & K, manganese, glucosinolates,
flavonoids

YOU NEED

2 teaspoons olive oil • ¼ brown onion, diced small

80g potato, diced small (purple potato is a nice option)

80g **turnips** or **baby turnips**, diced small • sea salt flakes

freshly ground black pepper • 20g finely shredded **kale**

1 x 20cm square sheet puff pastry, 3cm thick • 40g Cheddar cheese, grated

Heat the oil in the pan and sauté the onion until softened. Add the diced potatoes
and turnips and fry until softened (10–15 minutes). Season and add the kale.
Mix through, fry for 1–2 minutes, reduce the heat to low, cover and cook for
20 minutes until just tender. Preheat the oven to 220°C/425°F/Gas 7. Place the
pastry on a baking sheet lined with baking paper. Mix the cheese into the vegetables,
then spoon onto the lower half of the pastry leaving a 1cm border. Brush the border
with water, fold the pastry over and press the edges together. Cut slits in the top, then
bake for 25 minutes until golden.

BAKED GOODIES

These sweet and savoury breads, cakes and baked snacks are a pretty tasty way to take your vitamins and nutrients. Children, who sometimes shy away from the good stuff, seem to have no problem devouring these.

Soft seedy loaf • Cheesy seedy crackers
Supercharged muffins • Moist and seedy swede
cake • Guilt-free crumble cake • Berry burst tart
Zesty chia cupcakes • Chocberry cupcakes
Sticky squash cake • Virtuous brownies

SOFT SEEDY LOAF

Makes: 1 large loaf • Time: 1 hour plus 2½ hours proving and cooling

CONTAINS
Vitamins B-group & E, copper, manganese, selenium,
calcium, omega-3 fatty acids, phosphorous, fibre

YOU NEED
10 tablespoons **sunflower seeds** • 460g strong white flour • 10g fine sea salt
10g fast-action dried yeast • 40g honey mixed with 330ml warm water
vegetable oil, for oiling • 1 egg, lightly beaten with a splash of water
2 tablespoons **flax**, **chia** and **sesame seeds**, mixed, for sprinkling

Chop the sunflower seeds in a food processor. Mix the flour, chopped seeds, salt
and yeast, then stir in the honeyed water. Turn out onto an oiled surface and knead.
Set aside in an oiled bowl, covered, for 15 minutes. Knead and set aside twice more.
Leave for 1 hour. Flatten the dough, roll and put it seam-side down in an oiled oval
tin. Cover with cling film. Leave for ½ hour. Preheat the oven to 200°C/400°F/Gas 6.
Brush the dough with egg, sprinkle seeds, then more egg. Bake for 40 minutes. Leave
for 10 minutes then cool on a wire rack.

CHEESY SEEDY COOKIES

Makes: about 18 • Time: 30 minutes, plus 30 minutes chilling

CONTAINS
Vitamins B-group & E, copper, manganese, selenium,
calcium, omega-3 fatty acids, phosphorous, fibre

YOU NEED
60g unsalted butter, diced • 125g strong cheddar cheese, grated
60g wholemeal flour, plus extra for dusting • ½ teaspoon sea salt flakes
freshly ground black pepper • 2 teaspoons **sesame seeds**
2 teaspoons **sunflower seeds** • 2 teaspoons **chia seeds**

protects against
*cardiovascular disease,
osteoporosis & cancer*
• **lowers** *cholesterol*
• **regulates** *blood sugar*
• **supports** *vascular, respiratory,
& bone health* • **eases**
*rheumatoid arthritis
symptoms*

Blitz the butter and cheese in a food processor, add the flour, salt and pepper, then pulse to form a sticky dough. Transfer to a bowl, add the seeds and knead to combine. Tip onto a floured surface and shape into a sausage about 5cm in diameter. Wrap in greaseproof paper and chill for 30 minutes. Preheat the oven to 180°C/350°F/Gas 4 and line a baking sheet with baking paper. Slice the dough into 3mm discs and place on the sheet, leaving spaces. Bake for 10 minutes, or until pale gold. Leave for a few minutes, then cool on a wire rack.

SUPERCHARGED MUFFINS

Makes: 12 • Time: 45 minutes

CONTAINS
Vitamin A, B-group, C, E & K, omega-3 fatty acids,
manganese, calcium, phosphorous, fibre, copper,
selenium, folate, carotenoids, protein, iron and
magnesium

YOU NEED
400g self-raising flour • 1 teaspoon baking powder • 1 tablespoon wheat bran
1 heaped teaspoon dried oregano • 1 teaspoon Nigella seeds
30g mixed seeds such as **chia**, **flax** and **sunflower** • sea salt flakes • freshly
ground black pepper • 100g **baby spinach**, finely sliced • 100g **red peppers**
in oil (drained weight), chopped • 150g feta cheese, crumbled
2 tablespoons Parmesan cheese, finely grated, plus extra for sprinkling
325ml **soya** or dairy milk • 4 tablespoons olive oil • 1 large egg

Preheat the oven to 200°C/400°F/Gas 6 and line a large 12-hole muffin tin with paper cases. Combine the flour, baking powder, bran, oregano and seeds, and season generously. Add the spinach, peppers, feta and Parmesan and stir to combine. Whisk together the milk, oil and egg. Mix the wet mixture into the dry until just combined, then spoon into the prepared cases. Sprinkle with Parmesan and bake for 30 minutes, or until golden and an inserted skewer comes out clean.

MOIST & SEEDY SWEDE CAKE

Makes: a 20cm square cake • *Time: 45 minutes, plus 1 hour cooling*

CONTAINS

Vitamins B-group, C & E, omega-3 fatty acids,
manganese, calcium, phosphorous, fibre, copper,
selenium, potassium, carotenoids, flavonoids

YOU NEED

100g unsalted butter, plus extra for greasing • 250g self-raising flour

½ teaspoon ground nutmeg • 75g mix of **chia, sunflower, flax** and pumpkin seeds

½ teaspoon fine sea salt • 3 eggs • 125g soft light brown sugar

2 tablespoons maple syrup • 100g Greek-style yoghurt

100ml **hazelnut oil** • 2 teaspoons vanilla extract • 150g **swede**, grated

200g icing sugar • grated zest and juice of 1 small **orange**

Preheat the oven to 180°C/350°F/Gas 4. Grease a 20cm square cake tin with butter and line with baking paper. In a mixing bowl, whisk together the flour, nutmeg, seeds and salt. In another bowl, beat together the eggs, sugar, maple syrup, yoghurt, oil and vanilla. Stir the wet ingredients into the dry, then fold in the swede. Pour into the tin and bake for 25 minutes, or until an inserted skewer comes out clean. Leave for 10 minutes then turn out onto a wire rack. Meanwhile, beat together the butter, icing sugar and orange zest and juice until fluffy. Swirl over the cooled cake, then cut it into squares.

GUILT-FREE CRUMBLE CAKE

Serves: 8 people • Time: 1 hour 15 minutes

CONTAINS

Vitamins B-group, C & E, copper, manganese, calcium,
selenium, fibre, flavonoids, phytochemicals

YOU NEED

140g plain flour • 50g chilled unsalted butter, diced small

230g caster sugar • 30g oats • 1 tablespoon **sesame seeds**

1 tablespoon **sunflower seeds** • 2 teaspoons cinnamon

125g unsalted butter, softened • finely grated zest and juice of 1 small **orange**

2 eggs, lightly beaten • 50g **ground hazelnuts** • 1 teaspoon baking powder

a pinch of fine sea salt • 6–8 **black plums**, seeds removed and halved

POTENTIAL
BENEFITS
protects against *cancer,
cell damage, osteoporosis,
heart disease & rheumatoid
arthritis* • **lowers** *cholesterol*
• **regulates** *blood sugar*
• **supports** *vascular, respiratory,
skin & bone health, immune
system, weight loss, iron
absorption*

Preheat the oven to 180°C/350°F/Gas 4 and butter a 22cm springform cake tin. For the crumble, place 40g of the flour in a bowl and rub in the butter. Mix in 50g sugar, the oats, seeds and cinnamon. Set aside. For the cake, beat together the softened butter, remaining sugar and orange zest until fluffy. Gradually beat in the eggs. Combine the remaining flour, hazelnuts, baking powder and salt. Stir the dry ingredients into the butter mixture, alternating with the orange juice. Pour into the tin and push in the plums cut-side down. Top with crumble. Bake for 1 hour, or until an inserted skewer comes out clean.

BERRY BURST TART

Serves: 6 people • Time: 1 hour 15 minutes, plus 5 minutes cooling

CONTAINS
Vitamins B-group, C & E, flavonoids, other
phytochemicals, fibre, manganese, copper, carotenoids

YOU NEED
1 sheet ready-rolled puff pastry • 100g unsalted butter, diced
200g granulated sugar • 3–4 eating apples, peeled, cored and halved
50g **pecans** • 100g fresh or frozen **cranberries**

Preheat the oven to 180°C/350°F/Gas 4. Cut out a 24cm pastry disc, prick with
a fork and chill. Melt the butter in a 20cm ovenproof frying pan, sprinkle over
the sugar and cook over a medium heat for 2 minutes until it starts to dissolve.
Arrange the apples cut-side up in the pan. Cook for 30 minutes, shaking the pan
occasionally, until the caramel is golden. Remove from the heat and fill the gaps
between apples with the pecans and cranberries. Cover with the pastry disc and tuck
in the edges with a spoon. Bake for 30 minutes, or until golden brown. Set aside for
5 minutes, then invert onto a plate. Serve immediately.

Makes: 10–12 • *Time: 40 minutes, plus 1 hour cooling*

CONTAINS

Vitamin C, flavonoids, protein, iron, magnesium,
calcium, omega-3 fatty acids, manganese,
phosphorous, fibre

YOU NEED

125g plain flour • ½ teaspoon baking powder

a pinch of salt • 210g unsalted butter, softened • 100g caster sugar

2 large eggs, lightly beaten • finely grated zest and juice of 1 **lemon**

1½ tablespoons **chia seeds** • 150g icing sugar

1 tablespoon **soya milk** • ½ tablespoon matcha (green tea) powder

Preheat the oven to 180°C/350°F/Gas 4 and line a 12-hole cupcake tin with paper cases. Stir together the flour, baking powder and salt. Set aside. Beat together 125g butter and the caster sugar until pale and fluffy. Gradually beat in the eggs, then add the lemon zest and chia seeds. Stir the flour mixture into the butter mixture, alternating with the lemon juice, until combined. Spoon into the paper cases and bake for 20 minutes, or until springy to touch. Leave to cool on a wire rack. Beat the remaining butter until light and fluffy, then add in the icing sugar, milk and matcha powder. Top the cooled cupcakes with butter cream.

CHOCBERRY CUPCAKES

Makes: 12 • Time: 40 minutes

CONTAINS

Vitamins B-group, C & E, protein, iron, magnesium,
calcium, manganese, copper, phytochemicals, fibre,
minerals, flavonoids

YOU NEED

180ml **soya milk** • 50ml vegetable oil • 30ml **hazelnut oil**

1 large egg • 1 teaspoon vanilla extract • 140g caster sugar • 160g self-raising flour

30g **cocoa powder** • 2 tablespoons **ground hazelnuts** • 1 teaspoon baking powder

a pinch of salt • 36 **raspberries** • 12 squares **dark chocolate**, at least 70% cocoa solids

POTENTIAL
BENEFITS

protects against *cancer &
cardiovascular disease*
• **lowers** *cholesterol*
• **regulates** *blood sugar*
• **supports** *bone & skin health
& weight loss*
• *antidepressant, mild
stimulant*

Preheat the oven to 180°C/350°F/Gas 4 and line a 12-hole muffin tin with paper cases. In a jug, whisk together the milk, oils, egg and vanilla. In a bowl, mix together the sugar, flour, cocoa, hazelnuts, baking powder and salt. Stir the wet ingredients into the dry mixture until just combined. One-third fill the paper cases with batter, then press 3 raspberries and 1 square of chocolate into each. Spoon the remaining batter on top – the cases should be roughly two-thirds full. Bake for about 20 minutes, or until springy to touch. Leave in the tin for 10 minutes, then transfer to a wire rack to cool.

STICKY SQUASH CAKE

Makes: 1 large loaf cake • Time: 1 hour 10 minutes, plus 15 minutes cooling

CONTAINS
Vitamin A, B-group, C & E, fibre, carotenoids, copper,
manganese, selenium, calcium, protein, iron and
magnesium

YOU NEED

110g unsalted butter, plus extra for greasing • 110g black treacle

110g golden syrup • 110g muscovado sugar

150g roasted **acorn squash purée** (p28) • 2 teaspoons fresh ginger, finely grated

1 large egg, lightly beaten • 200g self-raising flour

4 tablespoons **mixed seeds**, blitzed to a coarse powder in a mini food processor

1 teaspoon bicarbonate soda • 1 teaspoon ground ginger

1 teaspoon ground cinnamon • 1 teaspoon allspice • 200ml **soya** or dairy milk

Preheat the oven to 170°C/325°F/Gas 3. Butter a large loaf tin and line the base with baking paper. Place the butter, treacle, golden syrup and sugar in a pan and gently cook until melted. Stir in the squash purée and fresh ginger. Set aside to cool for 5 minutes, then stir in the egg. In a mixing bowl, combine the flour, seeds, bicarbonate of soda and spices. Stir the treacle mixture into the flour mixture, then gradually add the milk to make a thin batter. Pour into the tin and bake for 50 minutes, or until an inserted skewer comes out clean. Leave for 10 minutes, then turn out onto a wire rack to cool.

VIRTUOUS BROWNIES

Makes: 16 large squares • *Time: 50 minutes*

CONTAINS

Vitamins A, B-group, C & E, minerals, flavonoids,
phytochemicals, manganese, copper, fibre

YOU NEED

50g **dark chocolate**, at least 70% cocoa solids, roughly chopped

50g **skinless hazelnuts**, toasted and roughly chopped • 40g **cocoa nibs**

150g unsalted butter, melted • 250g caster sugar

75g **cocoa powder** • a generous pinch of fine sea salt

2 large eggs, lightly beaten • 50g self-raising flour • 30g **dried sour cherries**

Preheat the oven to 170°C/325°F/Gas 3. Line a 20cm brownie tin with baking paper, letting the paper overhang the sides. Combine the chocolate, hazelnuts and cocoa nibs in a bowl. Set aside. Melt the butter, then remove from the heat and beat in the sugar, cocoa powder and salt. Leave to cool slightly, then beat in the eggs. Stir in the flour and cherries. Put half the batter in the tin, scatter over half the nut mixture, then spread the remaining batter on top. Scatter with the rest of the nut mixture. Bake for 30 minutes, or until firm. Cool, then cut into squares.

SWEET THINGS

*Sweet treats that are actually good for you?
It's true. These delicious desserts and snacks
combine the best of both worlds: decadence
and powerhouse seeds, nuts and fruit.*

Sticky energy bars • Goodness bars
Spiced citrus • Plum & cranberry crisp
Super sundae • Chocolate chia pudding
Berry dream frozen yoghurt

STICKY ENERGY BARS

Makes: 10 bars • Time: 10 minutes, plus 2 hours chilling

CONTAINS
Vitamins B-group, C & E &, manganese, copper,
carotenoids, fibre, calcium, flavonoids, other
phytochemicals, omega-3 fatty acids, phosphorous,
selenium, iron

YOU NEED

80g **pecans**, roughly chopped • 120g **peanuts**, roughly chopped

• 100g **sesame seeds** • 80g **chia seeds** • 80g **dried cranberries**

30g **goji berries** • 6 tablespoons honey or agave nectar

2 tablespoons almond butter • 2 tablespoons coconut oil, melted

1 teaspoon vanilla extract • a generous pinch of fine sea salt

POTENTIAL
BENEFITS

protects against *heart disease, urinary tract infection, cell damage, cancer, stroke, Alzheimer's disease, osteoporosis & infection* • **lowers** *cholesterol* • **regulates** *blood sugar* • **supports** *vascular, respiratory, skin & bone health* • *anti-inflammatory*

Line a shallow baking tray 20cm x 20cm or equivalent with foil. In a mixing bowl, combine the nuts and seeds. Add all the remaining ingredients and stir until everything is well combined and evenly distributed. Tip into the prepared tray, press firmly and evenly with the back of a spoon and chill for a couple of hours until set. Remove from the tray and cut into squares. Store in the refrigerator.

GOODNESS BARS

Makes: 1 large bar • *Time: 20 minutes, plus 2 hours chilling*

CONTAINS

Vitamins B-group, C & E, copper, manganese,
selenium, flavonoids, other phytochemicals,
minerals, fibre

YOU NEED

80g **sunflower seeds** • 40g **dried cranberries** • 50g icing sugar, sifted

60g **dark chocolate** made from 100% cocoa solids, grated

50g coconut oil • 2 tablespoons double cream • 1 teaspoon vanilla extract

Line a baking sheet with baking paper. Lightly toast the sunflower seeds in a frying
pan. Add the cranberries and sprinkle over the sugar. Cook over a medium heat,
stirring constantly, until the sugar has melted and the mixture is sticky. Tip out onto
the baking sheet and use a spoon to flatten into a 5mm thick rectangle. Meanwhile,
melt the chocolate and coconut oil in a heatproof bowl over a pan of simmering
water. Remove from the heat, add the cream and vanilla, and stir until thickened
slightly. Pour over the fruit and seed rectangle and gently spread out to cover. Chill
until set, then break into pieces to serve.

SPICED CITRUS

Serves: 4 people • Time: 20 minutes

CONTAINS
Vitamins B-group, C & E, lycopene, flavonoids, fibre,
manganese, copper, carotenoids

YOU NEED

240g Greek-style yoghurt • ½ teaspoon ground cinnamon

1 tablespoon runny honey, or to taste • 3 **ruby grapefruit** • 3 large **oranges**

2 tablespoons unsalted butter • 3 tablespoons dark muscovado sugar

1 teaspoon allspice • a handful of **pecans**, toasted and chopped

Mix together the yoghurt, cinnamon and honey and chill until needed. Peel the
grapefruit and oranges and cut away the white pith with a sharp knife. Working
over a bowl to catch the juice, cut between the membranes to remove the segments.
Heat the butter in a frying pan and add juice from the bowl, the sugar, allspice and
50ml water. Gently simmer, stirring, until the sugar has dissolved and the liquid has
reduced to syrup. Spoon the fruit into serving bowls and top with the syrup, spiced
yoghurt and pecans. Serve immediately.

PLUM & CRANBERRY CRISP

Serves: 4 people • Time: 45 minutes, plus 10 minutes chilling

CONTAINS
Vitamins B-group, C & E, copper, manganese,
selenium, calcium, omega-3 fatty acids, phosphorous,
fibre, copper, carotenoids, flavonoids,
other phytochemicals

YOU NEED
80g chilled unsalted butter, diced, plus extra for greasing

80g wholemeal flour • 50g soft light brown sugar • 20g rolled oats

2 tablespoons **mixed seeds** such as **flax, chia, sesame** and **sunflower**

2 tablespoons **chopped nuts,** such as **hazelnuts** and **pecans**

a generous pinch of salt • 1 teaspoon ground cinnamon

400g **black plums**, quartered • 150g **cranberries** 80g • runny honey

yoghurt, crème fraîche or whipped cream, to serve

POTENTIAL
BENEFITS
protects against *cancer,
cardiovascular disease, cell
damage, infection & osteoporosis*
• **lowers** *cholesterol* • **regulates**
blood sugar • **supports** *vascular,
respiratory, digestive, skin & bone
health, weight loss, iron absorption*
• **eases** *post-menopausal
symptoms* • *anti-
inflammatory*

Preheat the oven to 190°C/375°F/Gas 5 and lightly butter a 20cm round baking
dish or dish with 1.2 litre capacity. Place the flour in a mixing bowl and rub in the
butter until you have small pieces covered in flour. Mix in the sugar, oats, seeds,
nuts, salt and cinnamon. Chill for 10 minutes. Meanwhile, toss the plums and
cranberries with the honey and place in the dish. Scatter over the crumble until
evenly covered. Bake for 30 minutes or until golden and bubbling at the edges.
Serve warm with yoghurt, crème fraîche or whipped cream.

SUPER SUNDAE

Serves: 4 people • *Time: 15 minutes*

CONTAINS
Vitamins A, B-group, C & E, manganese, copper, fibre,
minerals, flavonoids, phytochemicals

YOU NEED
50g skinless **blanched hazelnuts** • ½ teaspoon vanilla extract

40g fresh dates, pitted • 2 tablespoons **cocoa powder**

a pinch of salt • 100ml coconut cream, plus extra if needed

8–12 scoops vanilla ice cream or frozen yoghurt

120g **cherries**, pitted and halved • 2 tablespoons **cocoa nibs**

Gently toast the hazelnuts in a frying pan until fragrant and starting to brown. Leave to cool a little, then transfer to a food processor and blitz to a paste. Add the vanilla, dates, cocoa powder, salt and coconut cream and blitz until smooth and creamy, adding more coconut cream if necessary to achieve the desired consistency. Distribute the ice cream or frozen yoghurt between 4 glasses or bowls, drizzle over the chocolate sauce and top with cherries and cocoa nibs.

CHOCOLATE CHIA PUDDING

Serves: 4 people • Time: 10 minutes, plus overnight chilling

CONTAINS

Vitamins B-group, C & K, folate, protein, iron,
magnesium, calcium, minerals, flavonoids,
phytochemicals, omega-3 fatty acids, manganese,
phosphorous, fibre

YOU NEED

500ml **soya** or dairy milk • 2 large bananas

2 teaspoons vanilla extract • 2–3 tablespoons **cocoa powder**, according to taste

80g **chia seeds** • **raspberries, blueberries** or **blackberries**, to serve

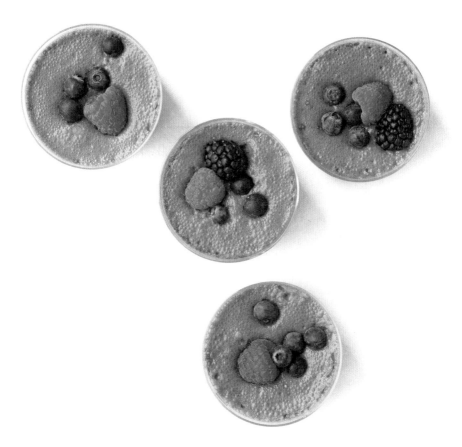

Place the milk, bananas, vanilla and cocoa in a blender and blitz until smooth.
Transfer to a large bowl and stir in the chia seeds. Cover with cling film and chill
overnight. Spoon into bowls and serve topped with berries.

BERRY DREAM FROZEN YOGHURT

Serves: 4 people • Time: 20 minutes, plus 3–4 hours freezing

CONTAINS

Vitamins B-group, C, E & K, folate, manganese,
flavonoids, copper, carotenoids, fibre

YOU NEED

450g **blackberries** • 1 teaspoon cornflour

75g caster sugar • 550g Greek-style yoghurt

4 tablespoons maple syrup, or to taste • 50g **pecans**, roughly chopped

Place the blackberries in a pan, sprinkle over the cornflour and sugar, and toss to coat. Mash with a fork, then simmer over a medium-high heat, stirring frequently, until completely broken down. Transfer to a food processor and blitz until smooth. Push through a sieve into a bowl to remove the pips and leave to cool a little. Stir in the yoghurt, maple syrup and pecans. Pour into an ice-cream maker and churn according to the machine instructions, then serve. Alternatively, place in a freezer-proof container and freeze for 3–4 hours, stirring every hour or so. Blitz in a food processor if there are any ice crystals and serve immediately.

INDEX

INDEX

ACKNOWLEDGEMENTS

I couldn't have written this book without the help and support of my family. Thank you, Ruby and Ben for eating vast quantities of leafy greens without complaint! I'm also grateful to my husband for being the rock that he always is.

Thanks, as ever, to Alice for her beautiful designs, Amelia and Victoria for the stunning styling and photography, and to Claire for her eagle-eyed editing skills.

I am also indebted to Magimix UK for the loan of a Cuisine 5200XL food processor, which helped me no end in the recipe-testing process.

Finally, a big, enormous thanks go to Catie Ziller for first setting me on the cookery-writing path – I will be forever grateful. XX

NOTES

[1] Di Noia J., 'Defining Powerhouse Fruits and Vegetables: A Nutrient Density Approach', Preventing Chronic Disease 11, June 2014

[2] J. Pérez-Jiménez, V. Neveu, F. Vos and A. Scalbert, 'Identification of the 100 richest dietary sources of polyphenols: an application of the Phenol-Explorer database', European Journal of Clinical Nutrition 64, S112-S120 November 2010

[3] WHFoods.org and the George Mateljan Foundation; US National Institutes of Health

Superfoods by Sue Quinn

First published in 2015 by Hachette Books (Marabout)
This English hardback edition published in 2016 by Hardie Grant Books

Hardie Grant Books (UK)
5th & 6th Floors
52-54 Southwark Street
London SE1 1UN
hardiegrant.co.uk

Hardie Grant Books (Australia)
Ground Floor, Building 1
658 Church Street
Melbourne, VIC 3121
hardiegrant.com.au

The moral rights of Sue Quinn to be identified as the author of this work have been asserted by her in accordance with the Copyright, Designs and Patents Act 1988.

Text © Sue Quinn
Photography © Victoria Wall Harris

British Library Cataloguing-in-Publication Data.
A catalogue record for this book is available from the British Library.

ISBN: 978-1-78488-041-5

Editor: Claire Musters
Photographer: Victoria Wall Harris
Food stylist: Amelia Wasiliev
Design & illustration: Alice Chadwick
Cover Design: Hardie Grant Books

For the English Hardback edition:
Publisher: Kate Pollard
Senior Editor: Kajal Mistry
Cover Design: Hardie Grant Books
Cover Colour Production by P2D

Printed and bound in China by 1010

10 9 8 7 6 5 4 3